A	B	C	D	E	F	G	H

D1610757

I	J	K	L	M	N	P	Q

SPECIAL NEEDS UNIT 01902 556256

X0000000094575

ALSO BY FAUSTIN CHARLES

Poetry

The Expatriate
Crabtrack
Days and Nights in the Magic Forest

Fiction

Sign Posts of the Jumbie
The Black Magic Man of Brixton

For children

Under the Storyteller's Spell (ed. with Rosetta Woolf)
Teacher Alligator
The Selfish Crocodile
The Selfish Crocodile Counting Book
A Caribbean Counting Book

CHILDREN OF THE MORNING

SELECTED POEMS

FAUSTIN CHARLES

PEEPAL TREE

First published in Great Britain in 2008
Peepal Tree Press Ltd
17 King's Avenue
Leeds LS6 1QS
UK

ISBN 9781900715980

ARTS COUNCIL
ENGLAND Peepal Tree gratefully acknowledges Arts Council support

CONTENTS

From Children of the Morning

Poems from
THE EXPATRIATE
1963-1968

The other world beyond this, which was longed for by the devout before Columbus' time, was found in the New; and the deep-sea-lead, that first struck these soundings, brought up the soil of Earth's Paradise.

Herman Melville, *Redburn*

'An old man bending I come among new faces...'

Walt Whitman, 'The Wound-Dresser'

One generation passeth away, and another generation cometh...

Ecclesiastes 1, 4.

THE PASSING OF MY GRANDMOTHER

She was a merry old lady,
A kind-hearted old spirit,
With graceful years and lots of talk;
Rocking in her famous chair,
A symbol to our household,
A legend of stories and regrets,
A fragile piece of skin and bones,
The only reminder of a past generation;
The years had masked her brow,
Time had purged her philosophy,
And disinherited her manners;
My admiration for her
Blossomed like an eternal flower.
One day when the sun was shining radiantly
In the heavens,
And a certain peace was in the universe,
She took a seat nearer to her maker.

CALYPSONIAN

You chimed sweet sounds
In rhythm and rhyme,
Music poured from the veins
Of your succulent guitar,
Intoxicated,
Composed in a sea of melody;
The inspiring tune
Shapes hot words,
And boldly evokes
The triumphant syllable.
Agile, jewelled vocals
Stimulate
The barn-dance brigade
Of painted colloquialisms;
And a smiling nightingale
Joining the revelry
Of your glittering voice;
Improvising on a prosperous chorus,
The island's angelus.

READY FOR A FISH-BROTH

They were laid out to rest
On slabs of greyish marble,
Embalmed in chips of ice;
All bore a look
Of mummified surprise,
Mouths agape
Eyes open wide;
I stared at them,
They stared at me;
It was Friday,
I was in the fish-market;
Later on seasoned in further crisis,
Perfumed with hot spices.
Broth boils through the bowels of the sea,
Fish-tea churning;
Reviving the vitality of the old fisherman,
And stirring the virility of the young men.

SOUCOUYANT

Witch of flying fire,
Creative in her pact with Satan,
Complex in her island's ancestry.
She boils blood in a barrel of molasses,
Melts blue and red candles
With the heat emanating
From her passionate bosom.
Vampire, shining like a star,
Scowling in the glory of the tropic moon,
Panting schemes of demonic orgies;
In her repertoire of smoky concoctions
She weaves seductive spells
On faithless, labouring flesh.

*   *   *

An old woman rubs red lavender
On her wrinkled face,
Massages her rheumatic limbs,
Contemplating the double identity.
She is known as 'Ma' in the village,
Loved by everybody;
No one suspects the evil in her carriage.

*   *   *

Night comes, she sheds her skin
Snakelike, with the venom
Of her tormented age,
Then she rises, glowing like a firefly,
Her fanged compass spins, she sways,
Rising, flying, encircling the trees,
Finally perching on a windowsill.
Corn the skin with salt,

'Skin-a-me, skin-a-me,'
Throw rice-grains in her way,
'Skin-a-me, skin-a-me,'
Count the grains, Quick! Quick!
Before the light of day.

TOTEMS

CANOE

Sculptured slabs of tree-trunk
Fashioned by the genius of the tribe,
Riding rugged rivers,
Breaking through devouring currents;
Skilful gliding paddles
Shaping immeasurable adventures
In an enchantment of chiselled tide-wings.

HIBISCUS FLOWER

The hedge fences the house;
Buds clasp, genuflect,
Burst with the flirtation
Of a cool breeze,
Yielding joyful red petals,
And the pious spike-headed stamen
Etching the pollination of a star-pitched home.
Through the feast of a perfumed sun,
Her warm beauty wheels the swooning retina.

RASTA MAN

Long time since...
                Chains exile him,
                Centuries divide him,
                And islands outcast him.
Long time since worries knotted his beard,
But the Lion of Judah roars in his head,
                Calling the sinner-man home.

YELLOW BIRD

Corn-bird, Corn-bill,
Floating frilly through the air;
Her yellow coat
Patterned to the sun's streak.
Eyes twinkle an illuminating stare
As she beholds
The straw-bag nest
Anchored on a stately immortelle crest,
Adjacent to the banana-tree;
She perches
And displays a ripe fig
Protruding from her beak.

STEELBAND

Drummers drill daedal sounds,
Stamp flaming instincts
In a volition of spider-webbed notes;
Harmony strained in kaleidoscope
Of pan symphonic.
The hammered fusion
Releases blazing, sun-breaking rhythm,
Ringing the steel serenade
From a bleeding emotion.
Drum-strokes puncture the sky,
Steel-pan tones sketch the tempo of life.

BRER 'NANCY

Flamboyant spider-man,
Spiralled sagaciously
In his web
On a cradling calabash-tree;
Strutting on the freckled corpses
Of moth and lizard,
And the windblown guts
Of a bumblebee.
His fragile potbelly,
Full of laughter;
Conjuring sorceric folklore,
Intuitive
In the magic of his living.

CALYPSO CRICKETER

(For Garfield Sobers)

The mood flirting loud applause,
Spectators in reserved hundreds
Masking cool elegance;
The batsman smiles,
The scoreboard skirts another century.
Magnificent warrior
Overwhelming the field with magical strokes,
Painting the scoreboard
With an array of skilful runs;
Three balls from the bowler
Go beyond the boundary,
As smooth rhythm relaxes
In composed physicality,
Creating ecstatic movements
In the sporting sunshine.

Athletic hero:
Flashing his bat,
Moving acidly through the field,
Bowling, fielding in every fashion;
Adventurous expressions transcend the game,
Challenging the murmuring horizon.

DANCE OF THE FOREST

'The poetry of earth is never dead...' Keats

An immortal rhythm
Streams from the earth,
Sprays the running vine,
Cuddles the swaying bird-nest,
Transforms the Jack Spaniard's sting;
The forest surrenders
To the consuming choreography:
Leaves balance shrub,
Fruit moves stone,
Flowers whirl, twig clings to trunk,
And roots reassemble, penetrating
The arteries of the butterfly's womb.
Forest rolls, soil gestures,
Sublime seeds evaporate;
The manicou, agouti and squirrel
Jig in ecstasy,
Greeting the frenzied strides
Of an impatient whip-snake,
Creatures expanding the flowering footwork,
Dancing away the fleeting gist of life
In the martyred green-world.

LAMENT ON A GOATSKIN DRUM
(For Kamau Brathwaite)

The animals grazing in the field,
Bleating 'Hosanna',
Insatiable and tame.
Hearts shudder, bleats slaughter;
Throbbing hands caress, curl, carve
The sunlit dialogues tuned in the hairy frame.
Animal: gentle, pious, obedient;
Reflexes timid, reducing tranquillity,
Soft tone-curves outline
The drum symmetry.

Sweat from sunburst armpits
Drips on protracted grunting goat-hide,
Intestines free from savage secrets.
The sing-song phrases resound across the village;
Voices quiver, voices yelp,
Expression beyond time,
Tears running through time.

Hallelujah! Hosanna!
Holy is the harvest,
Hosanna! Hallelujah!
Rejoice in the thanksgiving.
Cries reverberate;
Coal-pot fire warms the mystic lake,
Weeping shadows stir the sun's conscience:
Weeping at the glowworm's burial,
Weeping in the hurricane season.
Drum bleats compatibility
With the rural curiosity;
Rejoice with the resurrection
Of the primitive song,
Rejoice in the holy tremors,
As the coffin-builder retreats.

ABORIGINE

(For Derek Walcott)

1.

History is a madman
Dreaming he is sane.
Blood vessels spout
Mahogany-rain and sun-ripen juice,
Raging, washing away the memory
Of homicidal philistines
And ancient fortresses.
Cannibal teeth lust in the vein,
Rip the heart, then fall silent
To the plume of rainbow feathers
Adjusted to the necromancy of the brain.
Civilization,
Uncompromising in its discontents,
Has destroyed the treetop palaces,
The spontaneous jungle and life-giving volcano,
Leaving only the unconscious vision of language.

(Mind is greater than body, body must die,
But mind Lives forever in the wind;
Mind moves matter, transforms colour and movement)

See, touch, taste the purifying imagery.

2.

Life trails, flowing from the incandescent blossom;
We are not the ruined castaways of a race,
Our art lies in the splitting of the green atom:
The hidden language in the green rock
Generates the aura around us.

Alas! the madman awakes
And hears the explosion.

SUGAR CANE

Through the windy wheeling panorama
The succulent flower bleeds
Molasses-current spitting fury.
Slender sweet stalks
Bend beheaded in the breeze;
Green fields convulse golden sugar,
Tossing rain, outgrowing the sun,
Carving green faces
In the volcanic sun-splashed blood.

The reapers come at noon
Riding the cutlass-whip;
Their saliva sweetens
In the boiling season.
Each stem is a flashing arrow,
Swift in the harvest
Of melting marrow.

Cane is sweet sweat slain,
Cane is labour lost, unrecovered;
Sugar is the sweet swollen pain,
Sugar is slavery's immovable stain.
Cane is water lying down,
Water standing up;
Spirits fuse in the syrup-pot death.
Cane is a slaver,
Cane is bitter,
Bitter in the sweet blood of life.

PREACHER

1.

The city destroys
The tenderness of heart,
Holds the imagination in captivity;
Neon signs spotlight neurotic faces
Roaming the rum-shops.
'Christ Almighty!' bellows a pavement vendor,
Fingering a tray of ackra and float;
The city thrives on metallic anxiety,
And bony fingers,
Drained of comfort,
Scratch the towering concrete lamppost.

2.
Music unfolds,
Opens the dancing doors of the soul,
Opens the singing windows of the heart;
The sermon arouses trembling necromancy,
Each shriek is the expression
Of a sacred beast;
Sweet sacraments in allegiance
To the village healer,
Sweet prayers engulf
The slow movements in the bush.

3.

A man's language
Dissolves his home,
The expression roams the unknown;
A light falls between
The house and the world
Illuminating a way to his soul.

4.

The river holds the key
To our first kingdom;
The sea holds the key
To our second kingdom.
Swimming in the eternal reservoir,
Lives fettering away like gossamer;
After the golden ceremony,
Where is our island's faith?

MEDITATIONS

1

Bewildered bodies
Searching for minds,
Seeking lost personalities,
Buried deep in historic currents
Of the Amazon, Orinoco and Sierra Maestra:
Archipelago shattered by dividing torrents,
And tormented by archaic spirits.

2

We are the strange inheritors
Of a new history;
Inarticulate children with new mythology,
Speaking with foreign tongues,
Wearing strange disguises
And praying to alien gods.
We inherit dramatic ideologies,
Politics in wind;
Everyday losing the creativity
Of our phenomenal birth;
We hide from the reality of ourselves.

3

The massive silk-cotton tree
Stands like a god,
Mourning for the new Adam:
Extending roots to the prosperity
Of the new breed;
The flowers are bread of a new kingdom,
And the branches point beyond
The foundations of wisdom.

Feeling the strength surge through bodies,
And passion waits in a rural corner
Of the soul,
Waiting, grieving and struggling
Towards distant tomorrows;
The burden of admonished lives
Weeping on the perilous journey.
This is the tree of new life,
Flexing muscles in protection
To the confused forms of men;
The trunk expands along
The creaking, burning void,
And the leaves fluttering melodiously,
Hums a revelation.

4

(The tree-god guides us)
Follow old footsteps in bird-flight,
Foot-flights across heaven,
Seeking the seven kingdoms.
'Kiskadee! Kiskadee!
Rings the feathered echo,
The silvery song
Of a native shrine.
Dust to dust, ashes to ashes.'
Children of the earth,
Descended from the earth,
Spurred on by a ritual
Of splitting, crushing stones.

THE EXPATRIATE
(The Dream of Jacob)

1

The initial over-all impression
Is that of greyness:
Remnants of cannon-smoke from deceased ships.
Days are grey,
Nights are grey,
Houses are grey,
Streets are grey;
People are strange,
Intermixed,
Shedding ancestral plumes
In the smoke-screen of the green nebula;
Their total potentialities
Shatter the visual monotony.

2

The strangers blink
At the indigenous sun;
Black faces, white masks
Changing
In the apocalyptic fusion;
White faces, black masks
Dissolve the Amerindian landscape.
       (The butterfly climbs the ladder)

3

The storm breaks,
Raging elasticity,
Transforming the delicate land
Beyond the earth's subconscious,
And the miscegenated skeleton
Dancing to the scarlet rhythm
Of the aesthetic whirlwind.

4

The infinite reality
Of past, present and future,
Stand motionless
In oppressive sound-waves,
Waiting for the swelling torch
To ignite the paths of glory.
A cunning wolf scouts
The weary waterfall,
Everlasting flood,
Blood of the crawling brethren
Mutating in the timeless legend.
The destiny of purity
Lies in fading ripples
Of a watery flute.
Sprouting white light, dark on green fields,
Red flowers between brown moss,
And the lonely night owl
Hails the decorated landslide.

Poems from
CRAB TRACK
(1973)

'I prithee let me bring thee where crabs grow…'
William Shakespeare, The Tempest

My mast of love will sail and come to port
leaving a trail beneath the world, a track
cut by my rudder tempered out of anguish…'

CRAB TRACK

The crab's hieroglyph scurries the land
Like a hunter's runaway dream
Etching a signpost.

I see it here
Scrawling a map of the island's ancient scroll,
I see it there
Eluding the stinging ant-traveller,
I see it everywhere
Running my brain transparent,
I remember and forget the short-cut
home.

The tapestry of shell-feet traces
Landscape-poetry in hairy stone
Erecting a bone-pinnacle of the scampering faith.

Climbing the green summit, pincer spins
Slanting a leaf's eye, pyramidal scar
Skipping the bow-strung vine, twanging
Trapeze of serpent-grass, pins
An arrowhead to a mossy star.

Crossroads sliding sun,
Relentlessly the sawn light threads
The mountain-compass of a hidden world
Curling its tide of rushing toes, scything
A mud-hole spring, bubbles fungi, swelling
A toadstool tower;
Sometimes a mowed half-moon, bending,
Curves a skull-rooted Carib prairie.

The upright bead-eyed gaze, merging
The clawed panorama of world on world,

Footfall tunnels to spasms, scale-like pouch tightens,
Balancing the amphibious threshold,
And there! uphill, the waterfall
Sparks the chequered mouth, feelers veering
The crustacean trail spear-ways to sea.

CRAB ISLAND

1

The manicou-crab comes in the rainy season
Crosses the muddy river
And onto the bridge, circles gaily
Then charges the feed of garbage
In the seasonal rite of the tropic of cancer;
Its metallic back, jagged, deep-brown turning gold
Reflects in memory the sucking image of the full-moon;
Each claw spins in the wet earth: a libation
Rejuvenating the landscape.

2

Everyday the blue-backed crab
Journeys downhill in search of green stems,
Returning always in a wild scurry
With a hunter in pursuit:
Claws rightening track
Footfall tunnelling hole, fathoms down
Echoing through space, swiftly
She flies on crab-wings:
The crab-catcher slides
But retains his stance
Holding a nearby rock,
Then stooping in front of the crab-hole
Contemplates the blue-back's size
By measuring its dung.

3

The hermit-crab carefully sleeks
Its jelly-like body into a shell
Leaving its rugged claws hanging out:
Armoured eyes along the seashore
Camouflaged in sand;
Sea-light illumines the delicate image
In the sea-sculptured cell,
Through the fragility of its brain
The plumage pulps
A secret home in every shell of the sea.

4

The cunning race of crab
Scythes a subterranean track
Leading to the smiling sea-wife,
Hissing in the pulse of Neptune's sperm
Hatching the movement of the tide;
The crab's circuit splits the air
In a raw edged amphibious sound
And through a silver-eared conch
We hear an endless theme
Sharpening its round
In the rhythm of the waves' crack;
Wide and free, the shell-bound mariner
Rises in each shift of sand, trickling home,
Running proud on the scattered shore
Flickering the dancing foam
Through whisperings of surf.

CRAB PRAYER

The crab clasps its fins
And spurts: "Omen!" "Amen!"
All men are flesh without shells
Whether in heaven or hell
The crab-man sees himself
As a moving mountain joining islands.

Crab-altar: ripeness of mossy stone
Where the sharpened worshipper eyes god small,
Reflected from a clawed-out rock
(The souls without shells
Are becoming fishers of men
Shedding crab-skin when the moon is full)
The crab drinks the sea
And feels the transfigured pull
As heaven sinks.

Genuflecting on land, the crab
Blesses the giant, invisible fin-hand
Moving in the sea
The pip-eyes point upwards
Projecting the crab-sabbath;
Spurting water from its mouth
In praise of the amphibious godhead
Whirling the twin souls of crab.

Stone blasts rock, the swelling shock
Floats the crab onto its back
(God is everywhere)
Even in this bubbling seaweed,
Footprints in the sand, angel-hair!
Or a disbeliever, crab-catcher, buried there;
The fins cross, and a foaming sacrament
Appears in the sand:

Hallelujah to the sea where Christ once walked
(Treading on crab-back, the cross we bear)
That Galilee rooted between two suns
Is the swirling current in which the souls
Of the faithful dead
Desperately reach out for a human shape.

STAR FISH

The starfish shines its compass
In a surprise flight of fish
As the ocean unfolds creation:
A living hieroglyphic of eternity;
Interchangeable beam, streaming west
Rounding the astral crest,
Each wave on sky lifts a rainbow
Deeply veined in blue infinity.
The clasp of twinship light
Glints wild ecstasy
In reflection of a higher dream.

LEGEND

Old Ebby, the Obeah-man
Who lives on the hill;
The neighbours could not understand
Why the clawing-spirits haunt him still
After an exorcism by the priest.
It seems one night when the moon was full
Old Ebby initiated and entered a crab's skull
Then crawling down in darkness and rain
He traced the crab's steps circling his brain,
The amphibious instinct led him through a hole
Underground where he found a human skeleton
Clutching an ancestor-scroll;
From his twin-life, tangling, merging soul
He saw the separation and mystery of his birth
And the final fusion of his place on earth;
His racing mind could not contain
The multiplying creatures trying to explain
His lost life, forgotten for all its worth:
Then wildly scurrying through a cave
He squeezed under a stone-gate leading to a grave
And there resting on a tomb
Heard God speaking from his mother's womb:
Like father, like son
Melting in the crab-nerve.
Fused into one.

TEMPEST

Something like a prophetic blast
Like the gods raging in eternity
Speeds this green world in wonders of becoming;
A lightning shock shapes the living
Into memories of the heroic dead;
Thunder cracks, rain pours
The river of multiplying Calibans,
Islands peopled in the quest of the ancient mariner;
Hurricanes howl
Calling each generation by a magic name
And the angry volcano spurts a witchcraft
Of the language-sucking beast as the saviour of souls;
The wild winds breathe fire
As the broken empire falls in a landslide,
Then the earth opens with a grunt
Swallowing all unbelievers
In a sign of the slave's last hunt.

CATERPILLAR

The fragile movement, strained through time
Vibrates a flower
Lighting each petal into flesh
Repeating the landscape-streak
From the ripe heart of the sun;
Silently immortal in the green summer air
She curls upward, proud,
Prickly spotted, peeling fun
From the leaf's naked pulse;
The soft feet slowly branching
Sticking her impulse
In the imagination of wings.

FLY

The sugary head lit in silent ideas
Of the infinitesimal mind
Waters in sunlight, the smaller world
Above the shining hairy silhouette;
Buzz! Buzz! incantations of the shortest life,
Any moment could be the last,
So satisfaction fills her fast
Fulfilling a quick destiny
In every perch, suck-and-swerve flight;
The sweet pointed face needles vanity
Like the swift prick of a pin
Fading into a dark mirror;
Turning into darkness, she wipes her head
In an invisible light.

THE BAT

In the country of the blind, the bat is the beacon.

The dead have no music
But ants always bring news
Of the deaf singer drowning in the last quaver;
When the moon is in last quarter
The bat, sacred in eyeless flight
Swerves a G-clef in hooded genuflection
Drinking its sound in a dreaming mirth
Of the wingspan benediction;
One night the bat dreamt that he died
But when he awoke the world was upside down.

FIREFLIES
(For Shiva Naipaul)

Like you, I preferred
The firefly's starlike little
Lamp, mining, a question…
      "Lampfall" Derek Walcott

Every night the fireflies were our eyes
When we read the book of life backwards
Seeing the shadow of a name spelt out on wet leaves;
Our mother knew the longest, loneliest summer
As our father's face curved into grass;
Along the epitaph, the fireflies' lanterns furled into cloud,
A prophet's beard, God's smallest eye
Circling bad blood in the lineage;
A brother's annunciation in the new moon:
TIME WILL TELL,
Time will tell of the father's generation
Knotted in worlds beyond the family tree
Of the sacrifice by the mother-who-fathered-me:
The good-queen wife and the once-upon-a-time king
Carved out in ikons of the rich house
Where one day in a lonely corner
An epileptic great aunt thought she saw
Her jewel-box opened by a fieldmouse,
As she stuttered her sister's name outside
The wedlock of a son-in-law;
Time will tell of the long journey
Of the desired one, floating on a fired flower
Swelling the seeds of her spouse,
In sips of her father's blood;
The betrothed enters the temple
In the subtle smile from the reclining, four-handed god
And hearts rise in the holiness of the sacred cow;
The family's divining rod

Proclaims the dowry from generation to generation.
Time will tell of marriage:
The life of trust,
Security ringed by the male lust
When the ego fails
The passion is greater than the act
And the wife's duty is nobler than love's gift.
For love lies where the gods are;
Flames of venus, the fireflies draw the honeymoon carriage
To a seaside end
Where a fisherman-friend, soothsayer, worshipper of the moon's rise
Will tell the story of the pundit's fall from paradise.

HUMMING BIRD

The tiny helicopter-winged enchantress
Divines the eye through a magic sky;
Needle-beak pricking the air
Fulfilling the swooning flower
In a stretch of horizontal green;
Softly, softly, she swerves
Like oil on a velvet stream;
Climbing the sunlit caper, floating
To the finely-upholstered buttercup, her nest;
With the sun's kiss
She combs her breast
Twinkling an eye through a dark-blue feathered sleeve.
Loveliest at evening-tide
When day is ending, slowly, so sad to leave
And the green thrones of trees
Curtsey to the singing flight:
Wings harmonizing a dipping breeze
In Nature's ceremonial rhyme
In perfection of truer zones.

OWL

Night-sinews
Silently embracing the totality of all
From rounded eyes outgrowing the face
Softly plumed in darkness out of the haunted past;
To know all things
Is to see all things in their quietness,
Fashioned in the captivity of the mind;
Through the tree-house hall, he gazes into solitary space,
Falling away fast
Into the ravished memory of his night-surrendering prey;
Like a totem's majestic streak,
His beak treads the hot moon's birdlike wand
In nocturnal images migrating from the land.

PHOENIX

1: 'Prophet'

Walking through the sky,
Nature framed him
With a flaming cosmic eye,
Guided his earth-beam, spear-diving face,
Called him sweetest friend, star-catcher,
Deliverer, born of the divided race.
Behold the prayer, echoing in the forest,
Behold the star, giving light to dead men's eyes.
The road to deliverance
Is measured by the seven winds,
Whistling blissfully through life
Blowing eternal youth forever.
His flaming feet struck these islands
A long time ago
When he was called by the gods of the land
To preach the lost parables to men.

2: 'Resurrection'

Your shadow strings a chain of jumbie-beads
In the ground beneath your feet;
Souls stirring, ageless;
Your shadow speaks to the returning dead
In the blessed cane-root
Leading your footsteps
To the forgotten name in every crab-shell stress.

3: 'Fire Spirit'

Fire
Mothering man in the womb of the sun.
All things fall between memory and action.
Mother-survivor, ancestor-lover lighting
The glowing green in a fire of faces
In the spirit of a race:
Slaves rebuilding a broken tower
With a torch of burning flesh;
Then the forever-bride of the flame
Shoots skyward as the angel of toil
Re-christening the land, birth-of-place
Remembering the path leading to the temple
Of the fire-god.
This is the undying, purifying flame
In the hearts of the young men,
Naming the lost sparks of the sun
As family and tribe
Whenever a sword pierces the mastery of a grieving heart.

4: 'Libation'

...and here lies
Bogle, his battleground
Rhymes with the sun in the hearts of the young warriors;
His dream thunders the ageing volcano
Howling praise of the storm-coming generation
In seductive heroism
Of flesh built on stone.

5: 'Cihuacoatl'

Snake-charmed
Long sliding eye
Sleeking in the feminine smile of trees
As a gentle breeze rouses the curtain of maize
Groomed in the blood-baptism of every first-born;
On the horizon, the venom-light
Breeds its own flora and fauna
Ripening the libation in the charm of the light:
Changing skin, changing seed,
Changing God
In a twin-fanged worship.

6: 'Sunset'

Golden blood is the wine of heaven,
Recapturing youth from the age of earth;
Rivers and the sea and the mountains swell into holiness,
And the mountains depart, leaving the skyline gleaming
Beyond the circuit of the eye;
The heart-strings quiver
As Man dissolves into the soft rhythms of a flower
Haloed with new life, sweeping,
Consuming all vanity in the smile
Of the Great Spirit.

7: 'Jewel'

Spark divining the heartland
Conjuring a miracle in totem-stone,
Signpost of the homeland,
Here the Seer stands on the tallest peak of history
Vibrating sparks from the phoenix-flaming shower
In love and creation.
The heart's pure light shines
In the ritual rain
Wheeling the ivory's innocent eye
To the fountain of time-reflection.
The obeah-beads in jumbie-dress
Sprout landmarks of the life-giving jewel.
Blood of the oldest star
Crossing the eyebeam in a heavenly dance
Of cosmic flesh plumed in the dawn of the sabbath.

8: 'A Game of Cricket'

The crab imagined he played on both sides:
The shelled mind running around the river-bank
In circles of the land-and-water game;
Peering through the loom of the lizard's eye,
He caught a ray of sun, slicing
An alligator's back from the mirror of wet banana-leaves.
Crab-tackle, fish bat-biting.
Rising in foam; a slip-hook from the piranha's mouth
Twanged past the hop of the grasshopper, too quick to fall
In the school of tadpoles swimming out to bait
The squirrel's hind-leg four, squeezed
Through a breeze, like simply cracking a nut.
The cascadura spun his overs
In a trap of slimy leg-breaks
Closing a wide gap on the green
Where the raccoon would drive clean
Off the back-foot in a hunted run-a-minute;
Heaved by a yorker, the cayman fakes:
Bad light prowling the mountain-screen.
The crab perched on his mossy throne
Eyes the elusive armadillo crouched on the river-bank,
Ready in full armour to sidestep the oncoming landslide;
Then the agouti rolled the magic stone
And the river-world almost sank
In the melting eyes of the mullet,
But the giant crayfish signalled out-of-the-boundary-line
And the piranha moved down-river
Stripping the instinct of the anaconda
Who lurked in a tree
Jaw-bone-touching-water;
Down the gulley ran the wild deer
While the mongoose swayed slyly on the mud bank
Then drifted out to the mid-on perch.
Through the trees, coming in for a catch,

The branching manicou missed his grip
And fell, rolling in the slips:
Gestures of the anteater: the slimy tongue
Searching along the sound-barrier, windy wicket
Of the macaw screeching: Watch-the-leg-before-water;
Again the agouti rolled the magic stone
(Well pitched in)
With the river-world needing two to win
As the last player faced the slaughter;
The crab raced across the scene
Reeling on its claw
(If this hook-slasher fails, it could be a draw);
The mullet swiped, splashing its fin-shield
Towards the stone, missed in a sudden drift of wind,
Shifting the water-bed;
Spinning inwards,
The stone trickled under currents
Of the stumps, three shells knotted in grass;
The crab moved without a thought
Then quickly made an open-claw yield,
And mullet was out for nought.

9: 'Song'

In the quiet, spring morning
Confucius comes in meditations
On the universal journey
While the princess of the new dawn
Weaves silk from the silkworm's ray;
The gong sounds
And the Sages in the temple pray:
God is in the flower-boats' journey
Sailing as sons of the ancients;
Life is in the hands of all
But love is sleeping in an unploughed field;
Work is for the eldest sons of earth
Pain is for the dishonoured:
Fear is a madman with a drunken soul
Riches is a coward's refuge;
Belief is plentiful, like rice
But faith is rare, like the wise Emperor
Seated on the great ancestor-mountain:
Marriage is the holy pair of eyes
United in one head;
Death is the longest sleep of nature
But creation is the mind of God;
War is a graveyard of headless heroes,
And evil can be spelt backwards.
So children of Cathay
Wherever you are
On green islands where you have made your home
Your dreams sharpen the flames
Of history's magic crucible;
Customs and speech come and go
As migration charms the spirits
Flying from the dragon's mouth
Into the sacred lanterns' stream
Of the universal journey.

10: 'Caribbean Sea'

The rocks at the edge of the sea
Are symbols of ancient fires, ancient foes
And unfulfilled desires;
The sound of the sea, beating against the rocks
With sea-sculpturing charm
Is the speech of water-goddesses,
Riding the waves, weaving their hair
In a song of changing sea-urchins.
Singing loud and clear, their version of history
In a sad melody, edging the gill of the haunted barracuda,
While boatmen row towards a golden light,
Flickering a questioning smile;
The fishermen's eyes reflect a full-moon
Of blood, blooming a spirit of a terrestrial mother,
Who comes in the night as a ball-of-fire
Over the glowing green almond trees
Where the seaside-epitaph stones speak her name.
Around the shore, the sea-crabs lift
A curtain of seaweed rooted in human skin
As they journey inland on the memory
Of the ancient sea-charmer echoing through shells:
Behold! Memory skips on water,
Salt winds sting the mind, awaking from the long nightmare
Of tightening currents in a long lost tide;
We ride, and dive with the dolphins
Through a birthright trail of time-regained
In a chorus of ringing-bells from the lighthouse;
Our blood spirals this sargasso range
And the blue whale, our god
Lunges tidal-ways to heaven;
Our souls fight the age-old pirate curse
Tossing Aaron's rod
In waves rolling skulls in the watery grave,
There! Where our spirits roam

Each current riddling home,
The rainbow-crossing, bridge of survivor
Ghost-mariner, superman or slave
Whistling, woos the mermaid-queen, ocean-dancer;
Sea gulls swirl, winged on the eternal sparkle;
Plunging, the sea-queen foams
Knitting the gill-net map of islands
Haloed by a coral star.

11: 'Omen'

The firebird eyes the legend
Of the sun in battle across the sky;
With God all things are possible
With fire all things become one,
Compass of the past and future;
Blood of space watering
The stone-flower, earth-epitaph
Sprouting trees in the womb
Of the oldest tribal bride of God.

An Obeah-man sees visions
In the teeth of the rattlesnake, biting
Along the cane-brake, blazing sweet holy fire
In the homecoming landscape, carved
Between the skull and skin of the warrior-saint
Riding a tiger through a volcano of souls
Returning to time's circle.

12: 'Voodoo'

Tom-toms of tortured flesh
In light peeling the skin
In the name of an ancient truth
(Prophecy of the dead);
From the altar the priest invokes the god
Loa looming in the food of sacrifice, blood of satisfaction,
Mounting the brethren
Papa Legba, ouvrí barrière pour nous
Riding the worshipping spirit
Through the cabalistic trail
Of corn-meal, crucifix and flowers
Along traces of ancestors' ghosts revolving
Round an umbilical cord;
The god's horse wails in redemption
And enters the sacrament of the divine dance;
Drums chant freedom
On the tide of cosmic movement
Drums chant memory invoking rhythm
In the whirlwind of bodies trembling in hosannas
Wheeling consciousness in a trance with holy water
Advancing forward, fulfilled in the magic of the dance;
Drums rip flesh, possessed in a sermon of sorrow and jubilation
Drums smile, then explode in a gallop
Of ancient rhinos with a thousand names
Thrown in the voluptuous laughter of the universe.

13: 'Douen'

Lord have mercy on the dead, unchristened babe
Who passed away over the priest's wand
And must forever roam the land
Haunting the villagers for the name of its soul;
The weeping ghost creeps the dark forest
Chanting a lost omen: 'Hoop!' 'Oop!' 'Hoop!' 'Oop!'
Wherein lies the curse, fishing in the wind
For a name of the short-lived race, baptismal crest;
Somewhere in the night its mother burns a young flower
In a candle's flame
And blood flows,
Somewhere in the night the landscape whispers an answer
In slow blood trickling between the totem-eye
Of an ebbing moon;
The trees cradle their branches
In a prodigal ritual
Cuddling the love-searching echo
And the saint returns home
To a baptism of holy roots.

BLACK CAT
(For Miles Davis)

The son of the blues spears the trumpet's tone
In remembrance of things past;
The lonely voice howls a language, regained
In the isolation of rhythmic flesh.
The long notes wound time
Swelling the brain of the cat-child
Who paces the green apparition
Of a jungle labyrinth,
As its soul sweetly rightens, wild
In the melodic line, drawn to the brim.
The horn softens, fading slowly
And the jazz-son sails a nightmare, exhausted, slim
His tired heart, snapping suddenly
In the exaltation of the doubled life.

*   *   *   *

Licking the anointed hand
Of its dead master,
The night-cat drifts slowly
Through its green wink
To a candlelight spurting nine flames:
Nine cycles of birth and toil
Nine ridges circling oil
Nine names purring escape of the tiger
Nine masters bleeding in the blood
Of nine strangers;
The Sunday libation, black skin fused in black fur,
Cat-memory mews music, but the notes are still,
The world moves on, out of the trumpet's blast,
The jazz-man's will.

THE LION

The lion stalks in my living
Roaring my nerves into a sphere of hunting rounds
Where the one-eyed hunter (claws epitaphed on his chest)
Is the whispered meaning
Of a-river-flowing-through-a-needle's-eye;
Swimming its golden mane, I re-knit history, my loincloth
Remembered as sheets encircling an ancestral star
Forever swirling its perfection.
The naked ride soaring in death and rebirth
Framed in the hunter's cry,
Life is mirth, a jungle in the sky.

MONGOOSE

The dreaded pest-commune shapes the killer-season;
Rat, cane-killer, gnawing the yam-roots
From shoulder to spine
Gnawing away the roots of the sweet stone
Under the secret snake, venom-striker;
So bleak, the land shoulders its nightmare like a shroud
Waiting for the sunrise, overlapping clouds, dawn,
As the sly rodent, intrepid dancer,
Races the stinging nettle track.,
Jigs, and cunningly slides
In the shadow of the swaying cane;
Too swift for syllables, clinching sunbeams in its hairy fists,
Reflexes razor-sharp, whisk-edged teeth pouncing,
Trapping the sneaking snake in its own surprise;
And the scampering rat 'seeing death a necessary end'
Buries its head in a skeleton-dream.

One day a wounded rooster strayed,
Blood streaking the hunted track
Sweetening the hairy nostrils like magic in the wind,
Whipping down the gulley, circling the sly silhouette
Who reels and somersaults, gullet rumbling,
Tongue slicing its brain in a metamorphosis of taste.

Now the hunter becomes the hunted.

Traps over and under the hill
Ringing a riddle in every belch of the ichneumon-warrior,
As the squeaky soul reiterates
Each sin in the chicken-barn.

NUDE BLACK NYMPH RIDING A
BLACK STALLION AT MIDNIGHT

Nightfalls, into sleep's deep lustre, sacred,
The forest weeps
In the caressing omen
Of a blackbird's amen;
Night-sounds of love
From the dreaming dove
Talisman of the obeah-god
Nestling a star's eye in an ebony beam.
Peacefully, she comes, the dead slave's daughter
In the slumbering scape
(Where our souls walk)
Riding the martyred beast
Tripled in garlands of her face on dark water;
Goodnight, sacrificially sweet, meaning prayers
For the first sunset
When God sat in the treetops
Suckling the first-born universe
From the coupling shadows of her race;
The dark-eyed moon treks the ovary's climb:
Virgin of the cane-track
As the flower blooms in her womb,
Queen of the many interpretations
Of cane-root fusing her blood, sperm-crack,
Angel of many faces and places at the same time,
Sphinx-filled mother of the first and last warrior-sons,
Sister of the lost brothers across the seven seas,
Mermaid of the sea, where the foam rises
And thickens into blood, home
Of the mystic beast,
Sweet cry of the world
When the earth is silent
And the wind rustling the cane
Is the only sound coming in whispers

From a séance of stillborn infants,
Seed-blown, memorising the peacock's ghost
Flowering the night in the sanctuary
Of the beheaded ocelot;
The smile of the dark-eyed moon
Weaves a slippery phantom
On a wet breadfruit leaf
Lighting the snake's belly
In a bleeding tapestry of the zodiac.

SYCORAX
'Our Mother'

The zebra moves between moon and sun
But life is a bigger light
Rolling in one mother's eye
Consuming God in the form of a snake,
Hatching the earth-spirit in the womb of islands;
Her flesh bleeds the sun
Through the long history of divining blood.

Our souls take root in the snake's new skin
Worshipping her old and new hereafter,
Her arms, like wings, span the faiths
Of that first birth
Where Nature's womb was the playground of the monster-child:
Her son, our father
The slave-spirit in the sweet sorcery of cane.

She whirls the sea to the edge of visionary light
Motions her skull-bright ring
And each sea-fashioned thing
Takes on a human shape.

She speaks through a harmony of tongues;
Out of bondage her seed
Journeys the noblest track of the world
Where the earth is watered with sweet airs,
And sounds of her living-voice smooth over
The prophetic flood;
Civilisations burn and crack
But blood is thicker than water
Reflected by instinct on the crab's back.

The red plague drowns the conqueror's word
in the curse of the murderous plot
As the rough magic turns back upon his senses
The murky toad devours his daughter's virgin-knot
In the slimy art on the midnight road.

PAPA BOIS

Daddy of the bush
Sweeping tracks of the wild deer and agouti
In a ghost-clearing of the forest,
Under the demon-horned halo
Enchanting the trees in an exorcism of the uprooted race;
Vanity is a night-bastard face
Wearing a guardian's smile
As the beasts race back and forth
In the cloven-hoof's shadowy mile,
Trampling all sinews of escape.

Bush-man father in the myth of a shepherd
And the wild godhead rolls in a higher dream
Flowering the vocation of man-turning-beast
And beast-turning-man,
Delivering each other's soul
In the homing-call of the blackbird.

SAVACOU

'A Carib God'

Bird-bloomed
Where the saints sleep
In the beginning was the tribal plume
Elongated in ceremonial flight;
The prophecy feathered the horizon
Flowering wing-lit orbs,
Veins of the beak-fired root
Proclaiming the echo of a dove-call
Then vanishes into the echo's echo,
Whistling time through a star's eye;
Bird phosphorescence
Flares the almighty wind, thunder echoing
Infinity in the treetop temple;
Godhead caws
Starbound
Tightening the firmament
In a hieroglyph of its divine laws.

MAÑANA

Tomorrow, our kingdom come
In the sweetest earth;
From the last syllable of recorded time
And out of time, life is very long.
All our yesterdays
Have sprouted seeds in the spirits
Of the first-born on the road to tomorrow's paradise;
On these acres of sweet earth
The vines pull the heart-strings
To a tower of the universe;
Uprooted cane, uprooted silence,
Life is very long in tomorrow's memory.
Tomorrow is the world bursting forth in every flower
Riding on the wings of every bluebird
Dawning with the sun's first name: fire-bringer,
Phoenix-flower,
Light spinning our minds in resurrection
Of the homespun freedom, epitaph of the future.

LIFE EVERLASTING

I see in you, me
Dressed in the journey from Africa;
You see in me, yourself
Dressed in the hindu-shrine;
We enter the temple wearing the flesh of the world
Welcoming all gods,
Lost and found
Young and old;
I enter your spirit
And you enter mine
And our lives change the image of gold.

You see in me, yourself
The Eastern flame,
A million stars dancing in the lantern's frame,
With an interpretation from Confucius
I call you island-brother, name of a legend
Written in the talisman of the silkworm,
Treasure of the archipelago;
We enter each other's soul
And freedom comes to our world.

You see in me, yourself
Torn from a Greco-Roman tragedy
(Conqueror and conquest)
We entered the back door of history;
I took your grandfather's title
And measured his fortunes in the land.

Our voices echo in the crucible,
Together we chant our father's memory
As conqueror, indentured worker and slave;
Beyond this journey, the Carib path widens.

We are no strangers to the dragon;
Standing on the hill
We stare at the tempest and the flight from the grave
Then from Creation's well
Our blood flows to the life everlasting.

Poems from

DAYS AND NIGHTS IN THE MAGIC FOREST
(1986)

'– All the light here is equal-vertical –
Plays magic with green leaves and, touching, wakes
The small sweet springs of breathing scent and bloom
That break out on the boughs.'

A.J. Seymour

'The mark of the forest is on you....'

Nicolás Guillén

'...the land that once claimed their ancestors like trees.'

George Lamming

DAYS AND NIGHTS IN THE MAGIC FOREST

1

Upon the breeze
The hunter is invisible
In the spark of the kill
Of the golden arrow
Dancing in the trick of the brain
Of the holy tiger
Dreaming of tomorrow
Dressed in tiger-skins
Woven from the curse of the Obeah-man's jumbie
In a pool of life and cup of death.

2

When the sun comes up
Cane is the flame
When the sun goes down
Cane is the flame, lowered like a wick
When the moon comes out
Cane-juice is God's blood
Running along the river, through
A secret crack under the waterfall
Where your ancestors' stole a piece of earth
Etching a tribal name
Signposted on a stick.

3

In the pitch-black night
We remembered the unholy death of the Obeah-man
Coming alive in a child's laughter
Of daylight:
This is the magic fire
Melting blood into visions
Of a beast unknown, screaming,
Consumed in the legacy of the sunlight's
Neighing rhythm, centaur reclining
On the backdrop of a rocking-chair,
Where he sat on a wooden throne
Half-hiding from my great-grandmother's wrath.

4

Hands like mine
Are the oldest hands
Signalling in the search for speech
Guiding the calabash-cup of conquest
To my sore lips
As I drink the wild blood of my ancestors;
With the miracle of my memory
I make and break the world
In a panorama of mirrors.

5

Call me Iden. ...
And so it was I entered the magic forest
Tracing the blood-root trail
Of my twin brothers, Ti and Ty;
Our quest took us days and nights
In a sea of magic-tragic awakening;
Through a cave of skeletons
We came upon Nanny's ghost sprouting from an egg
Into the marooned day-night, in a secret hole in the universe,
She was pregnant with riddles, plotting her name on a balata tree.
Her womb was quicksand, sucking us into a golden throne and room
Of a forest-king engulfed in flames
But was not consumed.
The blood-root riddle wailing wrongs
Blossoming poinsettia seeds
Flaming wings soaring to a castle in the sky.

6

In this season of adventure
The forest is filled
With the giant Spider's cunning laughter
Spinning leaf-tricks into human bones,
His hairy face running red, as he spins
The sun into another kingdom.
The forest danced, sang, rooted men into trees
And shook their souls heavenward to eternity.
The forest is filled with voices
And the voices are filled with forest,
Chanting earth-equaking syllables
Waiting for the kiskadee's secret sign
Branched on the dancing cedar.

7

The lizard's wand waves
The ripening season of the new moon yam
Through the penis-root of cassava-blood
Etched by the swaying bamboo.
The land turns upside-down, all-seeing
In resurrection of Iden, Ti and Ty.
The screams of headless jumbies
Came up the riverscape:
Cudjoe, Bogle, Cuauhtémoc, Bolivar,
Dressed in old snakeskin
And caterpillar-light.
A jaguar swan-sprang through the raining light
And swallowed Ty
And vomited him into a scorpion's tail;
An ocelot climbed into Ti's mind
And sprouted hibiscus.

8

Into the grasshopper's hop,
We turned Time inside-out,
Our memory housed a dragon
Casting a spell on the iguana,
Swelling in full moon.
A boa constrictor circled the treescape
Swallowing itself, and spitting venom
In Baron Samedi's face.
Here, the graveyards crossed
Into the Aztec trail.
Here, the bush-gods' samba
Raises cane, hurricane, and Caliban.
Jaguar-man! Where are you?
Papa Legba! Where are you?
Oh God! We are dying a second death.
The sweet lingering wind carries
Our souls to the temple of rebirth.

9

The sacred whispering of immortelle trees
Highlights the changing face of the chameleon,
Changing into centipede, into millipede, into stinging nettle,
Into a tribe of douens housed in the echo of a name;
The bougainvillea salutes the chanting flame
Triggers the hummingbird circling the sun
And the musical veins of the sky-gods
Tuned their memory into bird-songs.
The children of earth are blossoming into truths
Of the brightest stars.
The magic shadow of God
Shelters all with a hunter's folktale.

10

Under the map of dry leaves
The mind is blown back
To the garden of the uprooted, screaming dead
To the river of vines, veins of vines
And vanishing eyes, all-seeing
Twinkling green and brown light
Into the firefly's night.
Between the bones of trees
And fingers of flowers
Lies the broken Inca's throne
And Toussaint's broken heart,
But Ogun swears all to life-everlasting,
Kali carries the mountains on her back
To the valley of becoming.
Under the map of dry leaves
The ancient winds sing sweet songs
Of the chameleon's undressing
Into the crab's cycle of the full moon womb
Sprouting three heads.
The ripening testament on a breadfruit leaf
Signals the mountain-king
To return to the hills
Where day is squeezed into night
And night is squeezed into day
And the travellers of one road
Ascend to paradise.

11

Exploring the cayman terrain,
Ty came bursting through the golden apple's grin
And thrusted his umbilical cord into the greenheart's throat
Feelers blending seed into Ti ablazed into poui-fire.
Over the jubilant green, the forest shook volcanic fruits
Into the laps of the bush-gods,
And Iden changed into a bullfrog
Jumping into the mouth of a secret python,
Disguised as a rotting log,
Through the green light exploding butterflies
And into the tapestry of rain-birds
Feathering frangipani on the altar of the lost Carib queen.

12

Soil erupts into prehistoric tricks,
Stones pelting skyways, charting heaven with ghost-bites;
Under the libation of mangrove movements
The mongoose strikes!
The banyan's cover is measured,
Stretched through sisal curling the parakeet-sun.
The forest's secrets are housed
In the guts of calabash, the sandfly's rage,
In the oracle of the night-owl,
In the spawn of tree-frog,
In the razor-grass slicing minds into fungi
And drawing blood from stones.
The deer is grazing on the grass-blood
Of man
Blown through reeds, squeezed into pollen,
Sifted through the sandbox
And blasted by the cannonball root
Melting into gru-gru palm,
Spawning tree-creeper, wings of wooden flesh
Riding the soul of the earth-goddess.

13

Deeper and deeper into the forest,
Ti tangles in a nest of lianas,
The crappo-wood jaws tearing his flaming heart
Into petals of pepper-spleen.
The bamboo creaks night of mahogany-armour,
Trunk-teeth piercing a green skeleton
Dressed in bark-skin
Confessing itself as conqueror
And prisoner of itself.
With a self-mocking smile,
Iden's head fell off
And rolled into a reincarnation of Bogle's head.
In the darkest eye of night,
A voice from hissing stamens
Called out: 'Praise the land!'
God's eye reflected on a dasheen-leaf
Spinning the dawning of a new day.

14

Shango rumbles the savannahs
Changing gulley-weed into wine
Of palm
Sacred where the hog-plum spits
And the tiger-lilies sail into drumbeats.
The new moon tongue tastes
The sweet sweat smell of Maceo
Lingering on the cypress-breeze,
Through the sting of ginger-lily
Opening the heartland.
The llama strolls in the golden landscape
Each step is an epitaph in the Aztec twilight
Where the sun rode the treetop maidens
Whose offsprings replenish Huitzilopochtli.

15

The jumbies huddled back to back,
Belly to belly, bursting sour-sop life-water
Into Mackandal; Ty sucked
And grew feet of eddoes, earth-moving,
Earth-searching, nerve-edging, Martí cocooned
In ironwood placenta.
Zapata calls the brothers
Into the tempest of mountains exploding,
Cosmos expanding with kinship spirits
Of lost and found companions.
The moon's almond-eye
Sleeks through Iden's bosom,
And the orchid's nerve-ends split
Into Ti and Ty.

16

Holy is the warrior-rite
Of seedlings sprouting Dessalines,
Holy is the sunflower mothering children
With pumpkin-sperm,
Holy is the spine-stem of Christophe
Manured in cane-blood
While Kali strums a sitar.
Iden dressed in ferns
Growls Maya with root-vowels,
Blows hurricane back into Time's vagina;
Holy is Nanny's feet fossil
Imprinted on Iden's soul.

17

The forest has eyes, ears,
And breasts to suckle runaways;
Every night a tree-hand fondles
Two giant nipples of the universe;
Every night, in rhythm and rhyme,
The forest's folklore cries
Tears of eggs into the worm-eaten skull
Of a warrior-chief.
Every night the dark-green foliage
Turns the jumbie-tribes into gold;
When a chord is struck by tamarind-harp
The forest sings of love and conquest,
Love in a runner-bean, piercing a rock
In a miracle of creation.

18

Ty walked backwards into history,
Nightmare mist spraying dayclean
Lightning the deity, fashioning
The orange-tree into smiles of an Arawak totem.
Ty floats through the forest's backbone
Webs the axle-tree in cross-fertilization
Of pine-trees swaying martyrs;
In the forest, there are hiding places
Where the hawk's jewelled haloes
Circle bleeding roses and palm fronds
Of human flesh twining Iden's leaf-skin shroud
In the brotherhood of hours.

19

Here are the hiding places,
In the skill of the cunning, crawling vine,
Multiplying the Karma of three trees
Rainbowed in Bogle's soul.
Here is the Land of Look Behind
Repeating names, lunar-lyrical
From Gordon's grave;
The tannia-root tightens stone
Into a homecoming sacrifice.
Arawidi howls through the night into day
Sowing shining seeds in dark eyes
Of sapodilla-light.
Names tangled and twisted in chains ringing,
Ringing Ashanti into Yoruba into Conquistador,
Ringing Ortiz into whirling magic
Of an undying flame.
Here is Gordon's grave,
Webbed by the cunning spider
Who eats history with pepper and salt.

20

Iden weeps raindrops into Ti howling
Rainforest blowing skeletons into shrubs
And the landscape calling, bellowing ceremonies
Of beheaded trees, calling the names
Of three old chiefs in the magic of the root-race.
Night catches Ty on the land falling, bark-peeling
Into daylight silver on green gazes,
Night spinning twigs into jewels
On a mossy sun.
Bush-horns blowing star-apples
With the singing winds of Hourucan,
Vibrating a harvest of resurrected choirs
Chanting victory in the green mansions
Of ancestors.
Ty is the night,
Ti is the day,
And Iden swings between heaven and earth.

THE JAGUAR

The jaguar growls words
From the holy weed rising
From the storm-driven caverns of your soul
Blowing your instinct back to Benin
And beyond!
The jaguar sleeps with kings and queens
In the embracing tempest of the tribe,
Licks its tongue in the smiles
Of the morning, catching flies on heat;
Sniffing along the glory of the sweetest smoke,
The sweetest awakening
Of prey caught in the umbilical net
Where bodies rise and fall
On the stalking-wheel of a continent.
The earth spins faster!
And signs are taken for wisdom;
The jaguar snarls fire
From Ogun's prophesy
And thunder crowns a king
Curling into tears and laughter
Of a new-borne babe.

A COCONUT-PALM TREE IN A HURRICANE

One day the island broke loose
Winds howled like a demon,
Blading the airways
Into streaks of terror;
The sky rolled backwards,
And collapsed in rain, lightning and thunder;
Rivers grew angry,
Uprooted trees ran for cover,
But there was nowhere to hide;
The sea's bowels ran red
Houses turned to driftwood;
But on a lonely hilltop,
A coconut-palm tree, waved, swayed
And held its ground.
Mountains danced, then crumbled,
Women chanted prayers
And children screamed jumbies running wild,
But the coconut-palm tree smiled
And took everything in its stride.
The men cried out for deliverance,
Daylight hid its face in darkness,
A cat barked!
A dog miaowed!
All senses were deranged
As the storm rode the mad landscape,
But the coconut-palm tree
Shook its head and whispered,
'Roots be still'.
The earth quaked, belched blood
Fuelling fires;
A tidal wave came in
Covering all, then retreated to the sky;
In the roaring, growling, upside down world,
A giant fist from heaven smashed itself on a boulder,

But the coconut-palm tree shrugged its shoulder
And held on to calm roots.
Roads showed bending signposts to hell
As the tearing lightning wrote
Epitaphs on a rock;
The landscape raged in full blast
Of the evil requiem;
Bodies bubbled, burst!
And minds were blown asunder,
But the coconut-palm tree stood serene
In the plunder.
The sky sucked in the sea
And rained salt tears
On the wilderness of human flesh;
The hills scampered and turned into clouds.
In its change of life,
The monster-season had quenched its thirst
With greedy destruction,
But the coconut-palm tree smiled
And spat seeds in vision
Of a quick revival.

THE RED ROBBER

From the depths of burning Hell
I came
Cast out because I raped Satan's daughter
My rage is a millionfold
My mother was a dragon
And my father a griffin
I can drink a river
And belch an ocean
When my name is called in vain
My belly blows rain
Flooding villages, towns and cities
I eat countries boiled in vinegar
Emperors and kings tremble
At the sound of my name
Snakes hiss! Wolves howl!
Volcanoes split fire exploding
Damnation scattering the sun
Watch me
As I devour these islands
Watch me
As I drink the Caribbean sea
Brainwashing minds hatched
From a rotten egg circling
The plague-ridden universe
I was the conqueror, slave-driver
And slave
My body grew in the passing
Of centuries
I can destroy
And I can create
Watch me
Reshaping islands from sea-spray
Sweat and grass.

CARNIVAL

The Silk Cotton tree
Dances breast-plated in rainbow-plumes
Into the arms of the tuning bamboo
Masked as a boa-constrictor
Leaping in feathers of Red Indian headdress
Swinging, branch rhythm curling pan-sounds
Punching jumping yam-roots
Wild in the motions of a breadfruit band
Garlanded in gold and silver, trunk reeling
Star-faces of parakeets in a sea of sailors
Coming in battling green
As the sky bursts
Into hawk-spray, raining yellow and red
Turning crimson onto beaten brass;
The hibiscus rises,
Sparkles into a diamond
Then waves a magic wand
Changing the prancing mongoose
Into an agouti with wings;
The Silk Cotton sings,
Beating a ringing melody
Through the heart of the bacchanalian forest;
The wild deer is a conquistador,
Threading sunlight with a spider's web;
Trees drumming, the road-march pulling,
Vines twanging tambourines
Spinning the blackbird's head;
The booming blast of trumpet-flower
Turns a red monkey on its head,
Winding into an emerald, jigging
In a purple-velveted squirrel,
Rolling in vermilion;
Bush-feet slap, branches clap,
Swirling a copper-helmet beaded in rhinestones;

The boar's grunting bronze
Blows ribbons of pink satin
On flamingoes clutching
A tiara of sea-green butterflies;
Harmonic winds caress the world-creating jungle,
The armadillo's gong electrifies
A glitter of peacocks coming through mango blossom
Plucking the humming strings
Of guava-flower ripening into samba;
Waves of coconut-palm cymbals clashing
Immortelle waving a banner;
The rolling hills chime mahogany,
Steel chords clanging sweet
With gold floating on air
And green smiling romance
Embracing a crowned serpent.

GOOD FRIDAY

'Bo-lee! Bo-lee!
Beat the Bo-bo-lee!'
Old man Brackley decided to die like Jesus,
Tied to a wooden cross
Shrieking in pain,
The sinners chanting,
'Come home brethren!'
Stones pelted the swooning head,
And the tumbling sun scythed the bleeding heart;
The Zion-wanderers crooning Calvary,
Twisting in a circle of thorns;
Brackley groaned and melted into a cloud
Stabbed with a cutlass.
'Bo-lee! Bo-lee!
Beat the Bo-bo-lee!'
Painted in blood,
His eyeballs rolled,
His shoulders fell into his stomach
And thirty silver coins fell at his feet
The brethren howled, 'Sufferer!'
But Brackley betrayed his boast,
Pleaded in the name of his holy mother,
Came down from the cross
And begged forgiveness,
But his wounded pride descended
Into a curse of hellfire
And laughter.

FOLK-TALES

1

The snake changed into a man
Changing into a snake swallowing its young
Into an unnamed river of caterpillar sperm
And the sky coiled into the hawk's bravado
Of the screaming infant
Kicking the universe towards one remaining question.

2

Man-eating islands
And islands eating man
Belching new worlds to conquer
In the hurricane explosion.

3

Yonder! Is the valley of the giant egg
Caught in the cane-spirit of uncharted forests
Where the opossum rides the landscape
Carrying the newborn on its back.

4

We come from the lion's home
Faraway from another home,
We come from the lion's home
Faraway from the sugar-dome,
And this long lost star
Shoots history through the jawbone of the jungle
Where dead voices of ghosts
Chant rhymes of lovers.

5

The sea is our mother and father.
Our roots are buried in the sea's garden,
Roses of seaweed, ocean of foam-flesh,
Light of red-snapper,
Heaved by the sperm-whale, spermed in the egg of shark,
Eaten and shaped by the barracuda,
The secret survivor in the splash against the grouper's teeth;
If we listen, we will hear our names blowing through the conch
And our spirits sigh with each wave's lash.

6

Jah says:
'Wrong-sided people never catch snake
In clear water
When mountain-top melting.
Trees planted in cemetery,
Bear ghost-fruits,
When mankind tastes the ripe flesh
And vomit blood,
Women give birth to cannibals.'

Jah spirit climbs the hill,
Tasting the weather with a lip-dropping raindrop,
Then Jah ploughs the fields
Making magic with red earth
And disappears into seeds and root.

Holy is the fruit of Jah,
Mighty is the tree of love,
Jah is the robust river
Flooding the wicked ways
Of one-eyed monsters
Trapped in history's rotting carcass.

AT MITTELHOLZER'S TOMB

Over the savannahs, beyond the window of the Carib's eye,
He found the charred bones of conquistadors, twisted,
Tangled between the effigy of a female skeleton: all
Passion spent in the fierce spirit of Kaywana;
Love like lust is satisfied only in the marriage
Of two alien minds;
The everlasting burden surrounds the penis and the womb
In the melting-pot of the Amerindian feathered dream.

Armour-wrenching, guilty without the act, hiding greed
In innocence, as the grotesque breeds the romantic;
Gold-thirsty through smiles of betrothal and betrayal
Where the slave sleeps with the master
On the smoking rocks of history
Bursting from the wreckage of a star;
Charmed by the spirit of adventure, this fearless
Monster is all mankind, released from the bosom
Of a jealous God.

In an occult signal of a fairy-tale full-moon,
His instinct searched the trembling hills
For the wife and mother of earth: mutations
Of the nightmare tribe;
Blood goes deeper than the sacred word,
From the centre of the world
A voice is heard
Drowning in the tumult of the first and last generation.

The blazing eyes see all;
Lover, pork-knocker, master and slave
Find themselves all bundled into one grave,
And the trees, rivers, and the sea
Entwining all in a living hieroglyph,
And a shrine besides
His flaming soul.

WALTER

Blown into the white days
Where all martyrs die alone;
Your body thrown through white windows,
Tuning the Essequibo purple
With marimba sounds;
The priests weep at the stone-altar,
While the shivering Caribbean haemorrhages fear;
Backwards, we dive,
Down, deep down,
Into the drunken fire;
Deserted like debris,
Landwrecked, we sing
Of brothers and sisters
Tangled in a faith worse than death.

But behold! the sparks from your bleeding brain
Light away the dread;
A candle glows from your spine,
And your heartbeat drums away the darkness,
Sheltering all under the umbrella
Of truth.

HAUNTED CAUDILLOS

Sancho, the bearded unpopular soldier,
Like a deceitful beggar,
Spied the sunbaked skeletons
Of the butchered cattle,
Bent forward, aloof
And comprehended an old cow's ghost,
Reincarnation and a battle
In the lives of humble people.

He began in mourning,
Shouting in blood-waves
Swaying against a daggered heart;
A politico of faithless improvisation,
Ravaged through the tenements of mockery and disorder,
At times forcing a smile for the brooding people;
He looked older,
Sombre and disgusting, like a worn-out clown.

With a mesmeric grin,
The new fashion;
His hanging lip,
A worn-out piece of skin,
As if pity could be regarded as a benefit;
His compatriots had murdered the poor old beast,
Making a feast with the flesh,
The firmament of conquistadors.

The barbarous destroyers,
Their names:
Trujillo, Gomez, Batista,
Machado and Duvalier;
Imagine the impertinence
Of these straggling puppets,
Taking life with pleasure,
In such wide and varied proportions;
Islands lament
And curse their foundations.

STORY-TELLER

(For Gordon Rohlehr)

Once upon a day and night,
The old man's voice charted continents
Composing dreams into flesh;
His head swan with alligators
And virgins grinding corn;
His vision fired spears
Into the thunderous waterfall
And caught a spawn of tadpoles
Spawning men;
Into his imagination
We climbed,
And laid our language-burden down.
Once upon a time,
The old man's voice raged war
On the mountains,
Baptizing every tale with a golden raindrop.

SEA SONG

Forever
The sea sings in the islands,
Wailing lost voices riding oceans;
The whale's siren swims in the trees
And Neptune's spirit splits,
Dripping flowers;
The lobster shapes human skin from seaweed,
Web of dark memory,
The mermaids are dancing
On the clawed tune of the stingray's tail,
And the melody of the shark
Comes in a serenading wave.
Once upon a rock,
A fisherman found a conch
Blowing a long, lost love-song,
Melting him into sand.
Forever
The sea sings in the eye-lands
Rejoicing in the magic leap of flying-fish
Calling all its children home.

The plankton's chorus fathoms down
To the squid's coral metronome
And the eel ignites a choir
Swallowing the world.

ANANCY ORDERS HISTORY

1.

Toussaint's spirit sleeps on this web
Of Caribbean cane-bones,
Creeping in the vowels of dasheen
Firing the sperm of Damballa,
Then raindrops shower the seeds of Caliban
Into warriors moving mountains vibrating cannons;
Here was the tribes' twilight,
Here the fingers of stars
Scrawl the dialect of survival;
Here, nations divide and unite
In the all-consuming fire.

2.

Then the spider became a poet
And a clown;
The moon whispered tricks in his ear
And he became a god;
His voice fuels the necromancy of the night
And his souls spins the tortured history
Pickled in the sea's cemetery.
Dessalines rides an ocelot
Breaking through the exploding brain of Leclerc;
The drums beating,
Firing lions roaring Boukman
Flashing landscape of cutlasses
Hammered into the sun.

3

Erzulie floats on the mountains
Heaving warriors carving their names
In the blood of the sacrificial goat;
The spider becomes a metaphor,
His phoenix rises into Gordon, Bogle and Bolivar,
Returning in the destruction of Great Houses
And the burning of plantations.
History is a black ghost,
Circling the islands
Carrying a sack-full of echoes
Chanting traditions.
The landscape does not forget
The conqueror's stumbling hand
Blocking the sunlight,
As the sea's salted terror
Bursts the sky-scape,
Thunder cracks the Atlantic
Into two generations, two worlds
Howling myths.

CRICKET'S IN MY BLOOD

Blood Fire!
Strokes in the middle of the imagination,
Fine slip-catch, stretching catlike,
Off-side, on-side feelers perched
Mid-on making style in the gulley;
Bat on heat, clash, ball bouncing century.
The play is a poem.

The play is a poem
As the sun rides the boundary;
Hooked by the torrents of slashes
From the sweeping willow,
The batsman fashions play
And the game swells the blood.
The mounting runs skyward, flood-board
To the scoreboard, stroke-play, turning, pulling
The rhythm of the day.
Dancing in the cunning cut and drive, spins,
Opens up the movements of the hours,
Shattering the field
Shattering the mind
In and out of time, slips to divinity,
Swings and shines golden
For the love of the game;
Rising to conquer, propelled by a gift
And a hunger.
The ball swerves, lifts, and strikes
Widens with pain and anguish
Breaking heights beyond the sun,
And the light circles all,
Screaming in the extremity
Of lives laid out bare in the height of sacrifice.

Through the searching trees, eyeballs racing
Challenor melting boundaries spurring Warner spread-eagled
Through Constantine gliding magic cutting loose,
Seeding heroes thundering Martindale budding Ollivierre;
The fierce sun reels,
Scatters a ray of fielders
Stunned by the batsman's plunder;
The curving sling-shot of Ramadhin and Valentine,
Mesmerises, and into the trap
The striker plunges.
Cricket's in my blood,
As the play tightens my soul into steel;
Blasted by the fanfare, the winds swell,
Headley wheeling the conqueror's wand
On the ticking time-bomb horizon.

Every night Worrell's ghost walks
Through the village
Delivering inspiration.

VIV

Like the sun rising and setting
Like the thunderous roar of a bull-rhino
Like the sleek, quick grace of a gazelle,
The player springs into the eye
And lights the world with fires
Of a million dreams, a million aspirations.
The batsman-hero climbs the skies,
Strikes the earth-ball for six
And the landscape rolls with the ecstasy
of the magic play.

Through the covers, the warrior thrusts a majestic cut
Lighting the day with runs
As bodies reel and tumble,
Hands clap, eyes water
And hearts move inside out.

The volcano erupts
And blows the game apart!

GREENIDGE

Gladiator on the battlefield,
Blading the landscape with an all-conquering sweep,
Lunging limbs jump and jive,
The sword-bat wields, raging,
A mighty run-running storm
Staging victory;
Islands somersault, spin, full-blooded, bounce,
Shooting fiery eyeballs,
Against a current of robust lashings;
Muscles snap!
Players pouncing,
Hairs split
And twine their way to a conquest.
Hearts rip! Torn into shreds of strokes,
Heads roll! Balls are heads where storm-winds reside,
Spectators and players
Beaten into the heroics of God
On the green ridge, smiling;
One man walks a tightrope
Tightened by a slippery magician.

THE SHINING BUSH

Light catches leaves in suspension;
The moon possesses with water
The glistening foliage
And drowns dreams in trembling grass;
Beyond the humid shadows
Weaving luminous secrets,
A cool whisper skims along fragile flesh,
Bleeding a curling sapphire;
Like a mirror, her soul opens
Into silence drifting through the ripening garden.

IGUANA

Perched on the edge of the world,
Dinosaur-clad, enamelled in iron,
Gazing prehistoric,
Time's beginning blasting time's end;
The whiplike tail-lashings
Lusting for long lost power,
Burdened with the age of earth;
History is caught in its helmeted wake
And the dancing sun-god triggers
The light of rebirth;
Somewhere in the secrecy of the face
The legend of the Sphinx resides,
Waiting for the homecoming explosion,
Blasting the monster-strain from all sides;
The mountains swell,
Gnashing its teeth in a whispering womb.

CHAMELEON

The morning breaks and changes into song,
The song curls and changes
Into the sun's broken teeth
Ripping human flesh dissolving into seed;
At noon, the laughing wind
Sprays a necklace of peeling skin
On time's nameless children;
The ancient companion of the land
Intoxicates the butterfly
Pruning bees into honeying birds,
Pulsing a rainbow of spinning language,
Enchanting the lizard's egg,
Hatching usurpers of a savage adventure;
Shedding tribes,
The sun sinks into the drum-skin,
Echoing wailing ghosts
Fashioned in the names of trees.

THE PUNDIT OF CARONI
(For David Dabydeen)

The ancestral country is descending in the cane,
Swooning in the sitar-singing daybreak puja,
In the temple-gong pounding Krishna into cloud;
Between the cane-sweep, the Guru turns
The July-rain into blood and cow-dung,
Measuring the land with mango-leaves;
Hanuman sits on a circle of rice
And screams, 'Ganges!' from Caroni to Guyana
In a hacked Sanskrit
Carving up the flesh of the Gita;
The pilgrims wail in the streets,
'Baba, come home!'
West devouring East
And the holy Star of India bleeds grass
Choking the birth rite;
In the river's sacred bathing pool,
The Pundit mutters an indentured mantra
And floats on a dark jewel;
In the evening, the burning sandalwood
Sweetens the stars scampering to a new cremation.

The ancestral country is sinking in the sun,
Returns in the yearly Divali,
In the marriage of the chosen ones,
And cuddles the closed world of the devoted.

But the Pundit laments
The faith drifting to the swamps of the ungodly.

A TRINIDAD JOURNAL

Measuring the sea
From this lonely rock,
I watched the wave's curling page
Spelling a speech bathed in bronze,
As the grouper scouts my great-grandfather's shadow
Coming in with the tide;
My faith is blown back to a thousand images
Leaping in hot sand,
From Carenage to Maracas,
Fishing me to the tree-top castle inland;
A brown vision of myself
As a walking-stone,
Pelts through the riverscape to Toco;
Wonders never cease
From the sea's beginnings:
Manzanilla wrapped up in seashells,
The lobster climbs an immortelle,
And the banana sprouts seaweed;
From Arima to Cedros,
My shipwrecked head blasts coral
Multiplying into mangrove roots.

Port of Spain hailed me as an exile,
My winter-blown soul peeled green butterflies;
The city swelled, burst
Into a million variations
On a theme of piranha
Eating the flesh of Adam.

Skyward, I leapt
Sailing on a cloud of a lost rhythm.
In San Fernando,
I cracked wide open, among
The oysters, I thought,

Some urban terror is masquerading as prosperity,
Some preacher's head is severed by the caterpillar-tractor,
Some village-headman is cremated in concrete,
And the sea splashed new thoughts:
Could the sea save the nation?
Could the sea drown the city's deafening metallic sound?
Could it save Cipriani's barefooted men?
The sea's voice roared the island's beauty
Through the mountains rolling back
The ancient clock;
Shakespearean syllables cannot describe this land
That once grew hunters and gatherers;
The fabled three-sistered hills have scampered
Back to Genesis;
Crazed by the moon's full face,
I became the green speech of parakeets
Melting in the hills.

LETTERS FROM HOME

1

The wind writes to me
Of a storm brewing in the Caribbean,
Raging waters and breaking mountains
Into dust.
I see heads rolling in the midday heat,
Eyes blinded by the sting of scorpion's blood,
I hear screams between the lines of blazing fire,
And Grenada choking in the eagle's throat.
The wind's pen trembles in expectancy,
Leaves bursting into tears:
A greedy giant is eating the Caribbean.

2

The sun sends me wires of blue rain,
Horizons littered with corpses;
Red ants gnawing a poem to the bone
Building an ant-hill of broken bones;
Through the tortured light, the islands crash,
Uprooting their dreams in a mirage of wealth.
In trying to become what we are not,
We are losing the reality of what we are.
Words travelling the Atlantic
Whistling drum-calls blading troubled waters
Communing with soothsayers and smugglers.
The sun's postscript ponders
Lost hopes and regrets
Knotted on a clothesline.

poems from

CHILDREN OF THE MORNING

'The weeping child could not be heard,
The weeping parents wept in vain...'
                    William Blake

STEPHEN'S SONG

1

At the bus-stop
Daggers hopped and dropped
Then the world stopped!
Writhing on the ground
His heart spun around
Regretting a journey lost and found.
His blood swelled a river,
Running through our lives forever,
Shaping a new architecture.
Calling a prayer, his pain screams
And the island gleams
A forgiving sound,
Stephen's song.
A mother's faith filled the scene
Sought to keep the world safe and clean
Free from untruths obscene.
The father's tears burst
Raging and flowering
made everywhere, green!

2

Shaded in black
From the shadows, they attack;
Knives bladed in cold feel
The sky-line; blood tunes steel
Into a sign from hell,
Belling against concrete
Streets running blind.
Through broken doors
There roars
A stinging wind.

What buildings might have spun the hand
What hopes might have graced the land
Etching a rainbow wide?
In the mind
Of an architect
Cement turns to brine.

3

Without the law Lawrence
Does not make sense,
As we ponder life in the past tense.
The bus-stop keeps a vigil,
And on lonely nights still
The crow sharpens its bill.
The women scream and spin
But will never change their skin
To lighten the shroud
Of darkness that always gets in
When someone dies aloud.
Faces mask faces in a white room
And with a black boom
An impatient song shatters glass.
Now, only mad men watch roses bloom
While the rest eat grass.
Night murdered the law
When nobody saw
The blades slicing stars
As the moon bled raw
Stumbling past boozed-out drunken bars.
Let the dead carry the sleep
From the eyes of the blind.
In the journey uphill, steep,
They stretch themselves and find
Landslides making mountains weep.

4

Skin
When the sun catches fire
And the needle-rays pin
Flesh into its deepest desire;
In the shade
True colours fade
Into black of the curse
Where the wave of the blade
Is ten times worse
Than calling a spade a spade.
London bridges are falling and bleeding
Where angels fear to tread
In the deafening ambulance's screaming
Where shadows wouldn't be caught dead
In the dawn's hungry awakening.
Only the night-sky speaks
With a half moon looking on
And Nature freaks
Into a puzzle of truths unborn.
Everybody seems to run away
Never saying what they have to say.
Sleep, sweet Steve
And give us time to grieve
Until we find time to weave
Your name into everlasting singing.

CHILDREN OF THE MORNING

The boy and girl ran into the future
And came upon bowls of plenty
Spilling everywhere!
An everlasting Giver lent a hand
Filling their stomachs from the land;
Waving wheat haloed their smiles,
Rain watered the fields, bright
In sweetening rays of light.
Safe from the hunger of the past,
They blessed bread at last!

They danced with the trees,
Smiled with the flowers,
Sang with the birds,
Whispered with the wind,
Jumped with the kangaroos!
Leapt up to the sky with the gazelles!
Flew to the ends of the earth with the eagle,
Then they became a river
And watered the fruits of the world.

SEA MUSIC

The sea is singing blue songs
In the great ballet of the whale;
The water's symphonic flight
Rings through the ceremonial light
Serenading the fiery red snapper.

The sea is singing waves of melody,
Weaving jewels along the shark's teeth;
A golden horn blows from the dolphin's leap
And the silk-black eel's guitaring feat
Glows hotter, swimming sweet
In the sea's clearest meaning.

The sea sprays tunes,
Circling the deepest depths of melody,
Where the humming barracuda
Flames the sting-ray's harp-strings,
Ripples coral violins, salt chords
Striking the truest notes,
Passioning subterranean moon and stars.

BARRACUDA

Killer-fish, the Rambo of the deep,
Fins flashing fathoms
Eyes circling the blue dive, peeping
Through the watery phantoms
Of its recent kill,
Out-gunning its own shadow;
The sword-teeth slash
Setting its skill
With the movement of the tide.

In the blue-green Caribbean yonder
The elusive hunter
Takes on man and beast;
In the subterranean war-zone,
Propelled by the sea's cutting ride
This sea-warrior fights alone
Spilling salt-blood far and wide.
The ceremony of currents nets the graves
Of drowned Caribbean kingdoms
Where the barracuda cools the waves.

SITAR MUSIC

Music curls and whirls honeying my tongue,
My head swimming in an ocean of pearls;
I bathe in the sing-song tiger of your caresses,
Cool winds soothing the hot breasts of earth.
Your ripe rhythm sweetens me in sounds
Smoothing the sun's charms with twanging fingers,
'Shanti! Shanti! It must never cease.
The magic star of India dances in my head;
Notes pulsing, swelling, bursting,
Fulfilling all my desires.

FISHERMAN

Bronze, fashioned by the tide,
His fish eyes blazing wide,
Rooted to the sea's paradise;
His smile cracks sunlight open
Reflecting the lost ships of ancestors swirling home.
The octopus' tentacles of stars
Reach his single thought
Of a rainbow-net of multicoloured fish
Whirling in the world-pool foam,
Brightening the light of his every wish.
He hooks the sun's compass;
Swimming, his head spins turtles
Eating salted grass;
In the blue-green-dark forest
Of ever-creating waters
His soul planktons to the dance of creation.

SONG FOR A POET-PAINTER

(for Derek Walcott)

His interior blazes on canvas
Mulattoes in the sun;
His brush-stroke words
Amaze sweetness on everyone.

Music feeds his whims
Blind drunk without metaphors
Seeding palm-trees so harmonic
All painters would sicken
Where light seems to swim
As the colours thicken.

The ripe grape of the sea
Violins his face red in the burning spray
Of surf-spawned simile.
The polished rhythm-etching landscape
Nourishes hot-noon butterflies,
Winging on song, thought-births
From the full moon taking shape.

In the pure light of plucking melody
Vowels re-write their sounds
Eternally echoing the sea.

RIVER GODDESS

Pour we libations of rum to Osun,
Fish-tail in holy femininity,
Breast flowing, mother of the river,
Sun blooding her divinity.

She rides milk-pure water
Rivering through the sweat of forest
Sprouting tribes round altars
Far away from home.

By riverbanks she weeps for Yoruba
Scattered through the Caribbean,
Tears her flesh in palm-wine,
Intoxicating new world minds.

Over the ancestral waterfall
Her swimming bubble-prayers
Free souls from the limbo
Of wasted years.

Water Mama, rippling the crayfish's tune,
Pour we offerings of blood,
Splashing love in the dark moon
Of the sun-fishing sermon.

Osun, mother of sacred waters
Bring re-birth to your sons and daughters.

OTHELLO IN BABYLON

His skin rolls off the blackness
Of the world crowding in;
He rhymes passion with bold rhythm,
The divine drums of his distant home
Heaving to heaven.
Horns staccato,
He shakes the city to pieces,
Devouring maidens, men and mountains.

Wandering into the teeth of battle,
Old, grey Iago's walking a tightrope
Without hope; he's surprised
At the rage still left in the white of those eyes,
As the handkerchief's noose tightens with each lie,
As that sword stabs whores masquerading as virgins.
Moor magnificent, more revenge,
Greedying out and in.

BRAZILIAN FOOTBALLER

Pelé kicked in his mother's belly!
And the world shouted:
Goooooooooooooooooooooooal!
When her son was born,
He became the sun
And rolled on the fields of heaven.
The moon and stars trained and coached him.
In the milky way,
He swayed, danced and dribbled
Smooth like water off a duck's back
Ready always to attack.
One hot day, heaven fell down, floored!
Through the Almighty's hands
Pelé had scored.

THE EGG PLANT

I stood between the egg and her
Wondering if gender was enough
To fertilize all the seeds of the new world.
God is tough in mysterious ways,
So the fruit grew divine between her legs
Suspending the sweet truth
Of the wild fire of her desire.

From stem to stem, we weave the days
Counting grass, and the wind begs
Me fly with her sun-shining sons.
The egg ripens purple;
Smiles and similes grow in her belly;
Stretching endlessly, she bloods
Through the earth-pangs of birth.

JOURNEYS

1

The river threads silver orchards of summer
Proud peacocks tread everlasting rainbows
Where angels dream of another heaven of resurrected dead.
The hottest footsteps coming through the valley
Print hieroglyphs on the roads of life.
The desert of Africa cracks like a belly
Slashed wide open with a knife.

2

Sailing the Nile with dusty smiles
Bronze heads shape new styles in the sun
Spinning sweat into diamonds.
Growing purer in the Ganges voyage
The lead elephant stretches the caravan
For miles, trumpeting the sacred call of love.
Journeys of mornings waking up
to the signposting call of the dove
Cooing all to peace.

3

On the laughing seas,
Through glowing jungle,
Cutting waters of sky,
Travellers greet the wind-songs
Welcoming sweet in sugar valleys
But telling of no-turning back.
Along the hills' highway,
Voices echo in lost river-beds
Where feathered tribes run night with the legs of day.

4

Along secret alley-walks
Shadows outwit the stalking tigers,
Scenting the trail with the blood of family-trees.
On the road, honey-rooting bees
Home-in on the tropical garden.
In this ripe pilgrimage
Bodies grow fat on the full-moon's age.

5

Africa and India wake as Europe's brood,
Squeeze food from the flood
Of the yellow river journeying
The landscape's sodden mud,
But still blooming

Deep, deep into the land
The legends stand;
Cobras with eyes of rubies
Secreting muscles of green,
Lions with eyes of fire
Sculpting black hands.

NUDE

Still life, silent as silk,
Oils the artist's impression.
An image of him comes through her,
Their bodies curled in shadows
Tightening into one.
Brush-strokes unclothe limbs
Into a sacrament of stone.
The eyes colour all;
Deep in the space of things
Skin peels free,
Slim, light lengthening.
Nightness is the dawn of the nude
Dense as dreams floating in a mirror.

THE BOY WHO DRAWS BUILDINGS
(For Stephen Wiltshire)

He dawned upon us
Pencilled into a child's drawing.
His fingers flashed through rooms
With smiling balconies to the sky.
His head danced in decorations
Of divine light fused
With the fury of a lover's cry.
His pen passions marble horizontals
Suspending granite with all his might;
From pillar to post, palaces tower immortal.
Through steel eyes, he ignites curves of concrete
Windowing stone mansions,
And tender as a baby's soft smile
He rises to the summit in style.

Iron-willed, steps winging to heaven
Shrining his art,
Stephen scales heights
Unknown and unborn,
Anxious to re-make the world
In the landscape of his heart.

QUINTET

1.

In the small drops of morning
The trumpet called Mama,
Its piercing notes picked her up
Tripped her across heaven
With a dream companion
Waking the gospel according to her death.

2.

In the heavy, cold morning
You came wearing the ice-folds of winter,
Your swollen eyes watering,
Your nose smearing across the mirror,
Your memory failing
As the snow-winds sail
Across irises going blind.
In the sung version of your life
Every day was a broken song.
With all that sorrow
How could you reach tomorrow,
Tune the trumpet into gold?

3.

The moth-lady pampers flame
In the night-fruit of her skin.
She flutters songs, burning her
Garments of passion,
Teasing sparks trapped in a bubble
Until suddenly the night blows asunder
And she perishes, eternally free.

4.

Woman, the magic of creation,
Voyages to her sensation
Light-years away from her real love;
In an intoxicating serenade
Eternal Mother confesses her curse,
The grinding seeds of guitars
Croon in her womb and give birth
To rhumbas knifing empires.
In the dark history of her face,
Her pace grounded mankind to a halt
Striving to out-fox the wolf-pack of her race.

5.

Drums dagger the heart
Stretched beyond rhythms
At the nerve-end of the virtuoso's art.
All year round the sun sings its hot symphony
And the wave-strumming of sea-songs
Compose the islands larger than life
With the tuned skill of the fishermen's knives.
The chords burst in their heated climb,
But only five notes feed the sweet steel violin
Rhyming the fingers of time.

ABOUT THE AUTHOR

Faustin Charles was born in Trinidad in 1944 and his passion for writing started when he was still at school. As there were then no publishing houses in the Caribbean, he came to the conclusion that he would have to move to Britain or the United States in order to have a career.

He has been regularly published since 1969 but has not confined his talents to the written word. He is passionate about the culture, myths and folktales of the whole Caribbean area and has worked tirelessly to promote knowledge, interest and understanding amongst ex-patriots and his adopted countrymen alike.

He worked as the Community Literacy Officer in Enfield and encouraged many youngsters to realise the richness and pleasure of the written word. He undertakes freelance engagements of storytelling and poetry reading and has enjoyed such diverse appointments as a creative writing fellowship at Warwick University and the writer in residence at Wormwood Scrubs. He is a charismatic and compelling storyteller touring schools and community venues.

He has published three collections of poetry and his work is in all the major anthologies of Caribbean verse. He has published two adult novel *Sign Posts of the Jumbie* and *The Black Magic Man of Brixton*.

More recently he has built a successful career as a writer for children, publishing both poems and stories with publishing houses such as Longmans, Penguin and Bloomsbury. His *The Selfish Crocodile* has now sold over 250,000 copies.

'Faustin Charles offers an utterance of his own, which promises to push the frontier of West Indian expression in poetry one understanding further on'
Kamau Brathwaite.

'Faustin Charles' work seems to me outstandingly successful in capturing certain essentially West Indian qualities – the mixture of European and African cultures, of the bizarre and the beautiful, the grotesque and the sinister. The "climate of the heart", which West Indians know of but cannot always communicate, speaks clearly and delicately in his work.'
Edward Lucie-Smith.

NEW POETRY FROM PEEPAL TREE

Anthony Kellman
Limestone: an epic poem of Barbados
ISBN: 9781845230036; pp. 203; 2008; £9.99

Limestone is the epic of Barbados. Drawing on the rhythms of the Tuk or ruk-a-tuk bands, Anthony Kellman employs specifically Barbadian verse forms to tell the story of the island from the genocide of the Amerindian, up to the present day.

Through a web of the voices and stories of invented and actual historical figures, through moments of high drama and a lyrical eye for the undertones of social change, *Limestone* explores the contradictory richness of what it means to be Barbadian.

It tells how English colonists, white indentured labourers, absentee planters and African slaves shaped the island's often violent beginnings and probes beyond the historical record to explore the inner motivations of figures such as Anna Fortuna, betrayer of Cuffee's rebellion, and Bussa and Nanny Grigg, leaders of the 1816 revolt.

Through the stories of the exiled African King Jaja, the confederacy riots of 1876 and the Clement Payne rebellion of 1937, *Limestone* records the people's unquenchable desire for freedom, whilst through the voices of those who led the constitutional struggle against colonialism – in particular Grantley Adams and Errol Barrow – Kellman explores the temptations of personal power and the anguish of reluctant compromise. And as the queues of would-be emigrants at the American consulate lengthen, the poem asks: who has benefited from the people's struggles of the past?

Limestone also tells the stories of Livingstone, a young musician, and Levinia, a teacher, who meet when the return to Barbados from abroad. Their stories explore the complex relationship of many contemporary Barbadians to their homeland: deep attachment and an equal frustration over the absence of opportunities.

Fourteen years in the making, *Limestone* is never other than a poem: a treasure house of image, sound and rhythm that moves, entertains and absorbs the reader in its world.

Earl McKenzie
The Almond Leaf
ISBN: 9781845230128; pp. 64; 2008; £7.99

Earl McKenzie's poems are beautifully and deceptively simple, but their crystalline observations record life in all its complexity. Patricia Harkins, in *The Caribbean Writer* described his earlier *Against Linearity* as a 'book to cherish' for the particularity of its images from nature and 'his keen insight into human hearts'.

These qualities are deepened in this new collection, where the whiff of mortality demands an even stronger sense of continuance, affirmation and joy in love, family, music, art and, above all, in his beloved Jamaica. If this Eden is a fallen one, Adam has not been expelled from the garden where, with his mate, 'Together/we share the temptation of the snake/in the garden of rocks and flowers'.

In these poems of quirky, unassuming observations, McKenzie never preaches, but he does find sermons in lilies, and what he discovers for himself provides a way of wisdom for those readers inclined to look for it.

All Peepal Tree titles are available from the website
www.peepaltreepress.com
with a money back guarantee, secure credit card ordering
and fast delivery throughout the world at cost or less.

Peepal Tree Press is celebrated as the home of challenging and inspiring literature from the Caribbean and Black Britain. Visit www.peepaltreepress.com to read sample poems and reviews, discover new authors, established names and access a wealth of information. Subscribe to our mailing list for news of new books and events.

Contact us at:
Peepal Tree Press, 17 King's Avenue, Leeds LS6 1QS, UK
Tel: +44 (0) 113 245 1703 E-mail: contact@peepaltreepress.com